JANE FELTH

PERUVIAN TEXTILES

SHIRE ETHNOGRAPHY

2

Cover photograph
A woman weaving warp-striped cloth on a backstrap loom near Cuzco. She is inserting a long shuttle into the shed. On the ground in front of her lie a weaving sword and a spindle. Another weaving sword, heddle rod and shed rod can be seen in the loom.
(Photograph: Rosalie Gotch.)

In memory of Lynn Feltham

British Library Cataloguing in Publication Data:

Published by
SHIRE PUBLICATIONS LTD
Cromwell House, Church Street, Princes Risborough,
Aylesbury, Bucks HP17 9AJ, UK.

Series Editor: Bryan Cranstone

ISBN 0 7478 0014 6

First published 1989

Printed in Great Britain by
C. I. Thomas & Sons (Haverfordwest) Ltd,
Press Buildings, Merlins Bridge, Haverfordwest, Dyfed SA61 1XF.

Contents

Acknowledgements

Space does not permit me to thank individually all those who have contributed to this book by their ideas, suggestions and in smoothing my path, especially those working in museums. I should like to give particular thanks to the staff of the Birmingham Museum and Art Gallery, the Bolton Museum and Art Gallery, the Bristol Museum and Art Gallery, the Cambridge University Museum of Archaeology and Anthropology, the Liverpool Museum, the Manchester Museum, the Pitt Rivers Museum and the Victoria and Albert Museum. In the United States the staff of the American Museum of Natural History and the Textile Museum have been most helpful. Finally, my special gratitude to Rosalie Gotch, Jonathan Hill, Rodrick Owen, Anne Paul and James Vreeland.

4

List of illustrations

Preface

The study of Peruvian textiles belongs properly to the twentieth century for, although the Spanish chroniclers were impressed with the sumptuous garments they saw, they did little to preserve them or to record how they were made. During the Colonial Period weaving on indigenous looms declined, notably on the coast, since there was no longer an outlet for the kind of cloth that such looms had produced in the past: the Inca and local nobility had adopted Spanish dress and native rituals involving textile offerings had been forbidden. Highland Indians continued to make cloth for their own personal use, but no one except its makers valued it.

Then, in the nineteenth century, travellers from Europe and North America visited the new South American republics and published descriptions of their antiquities, including textiles, which they had obtained from pothunters or from their own amateur digging on the easily accessible coast around Lima. Their finds were donated to Western museums and exhibited. In the last quarter of the same century German archaeologists like Wilhelm Reiss, Alphons Stübel and Max Uhle undertook scientific excavations at Ancón and Pachacámac and published detailed drawings and photographs of the textiles they found in mummy bundles. These and other publications, together with the museum exhibits, aroused public interest since examples of Old World early textiles were rare. During the twentieth century, as archaeology and anthropology expanded in the Americas, the provenance of these archaeological textiles was better documented and temporal, areal and iconographic differences became apparent, enabling the development of ancient weaving to be outlined. Interest in ethnographic textiles was slower to gain momentum until the late 1960s and the advent of mass tourism, by which time it had been realised that studies of contemporary methods of spinning, dyeing and weaving could elucidate those of antiquity.

The dry climate of the Peruvian coast has preserved ancient textiles from graves of most prehistoric periods. Unfortunately, however, there is little indigenous weaving on the coast today, except for a few cotton articles produced in the far north of Peru and Ecuador. Therefore one must go to the highlands of these countries and to Bolivia, where such weaving still flourishes, in order to examine contemporary techniques. On the other hand, the damp climate of the highlands has not preserved ancient textiles, so our best clues to the development of weaving in that zone are certain pieces from coastal graves that are entirely of wool and whose structure and designs relate them to the modern highland weaving tradition. By comparing the products of both zones, and the ancient with the modern, we are able to fill in the gaps in our knowledge of the history of Peruvian weaving.

For the purposes of this book, the Peru of the title refers to that part of the central Andes conquered by the Incas and called by them Tawantinsuyu. Thus, it excludes the tropical forest in the east of the modern republic of Peru, but includes parts of Chile, Argentina, Bolivia and Ecuador. This area is the homeland of the modern Quechua-speaking and Aymara-speaking Indians. It is divided into coast and highlands. The former refers to the narrow strip of desert running along the shore from the Gulf of Guayaquil to the Atacama Desert in north Chile and to the interior of valleys with westward-flowing rivers, from sea level to 1500 metres (5000 feet). Land above this altitude is known as highlands.

I have chosen to deal with a long timespan, from 8500 BC to the present, because the modern textiles are heirs to pre-columbian traditions despite the obvious cultural changes brought about by the Spanish conquest and industrial society. Moreover, only in Peru is it possible to trace the history of cloth production from its earliest beginnings to the present. Because of this wide areal and temporal coverage, I have concentrated on loom-woven textiles and made only slight mention of braiding, looping, knotted netting and other techniques. The interested reader can pursue the study of these in one of the books listed for further reading. Two other points should be noted. Unless stated to the contrary, wool refers to camelid wool, that is the spun hairs of the llama, alpaca and vicuña, a group of South American mammals related to Asian camels; the warps are orientated vertically in the figures and warp measurements are given first in the accompanying captions.

Chronology

The prehistory of the Central Andes is usually set in a framework of periods developed by North American archaeologists. In general horizons occur when a single art style spread to many areas. Intervening periods are when local styles flourished.

	12000	
Early Preceramic		Man living in Central Andes as hunter and gatherer.
	4000 BC	
Late Preceramic		Domestication of plants and animals.
	2000 BC	
Initial Period		Introduction of pottery and heddle loom.
	1400 BC	
Early Horizon		Spread of style associated with stone carvings at Chavín de Huántar.
	400 BC	
Early Intermediate Period		Moche, Nazca and Tiahuanaco become centres of importance.
	AD 500	
Middle Horizon		Spread of style associated with stone carvings at Tiahuanaco via site of Wari.
	AD 900	
Late Intermediate Period		Expansion of Chimú kingdom on the coast. Rise of the Incas in the highlands.
	AD 1476	
Late Horizon		Inca conquest of central and south coasts.
	AD 1532	
Colonial Period		Arrival of Spaniards. Conquest of Peru. Rapid depopulation of coast and some parts of highlands.
	AD 1824	
Republican Period		Battle of Ayacucho frees Peru and Bolivia from Spanish domination.
	present	

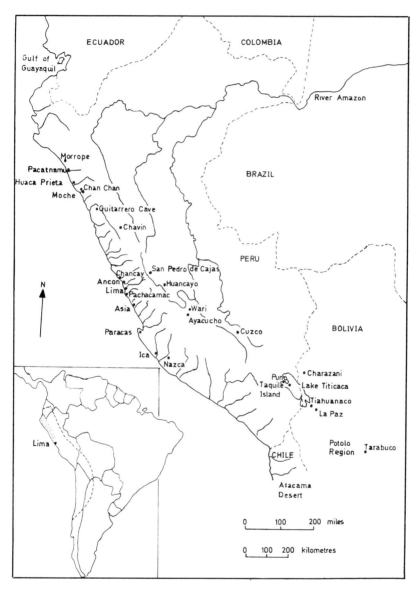

1. Map of the Central Andes showing the places mentioned in the text. Inset is a map of South America showing the extent of the Inca empire (dashed line) and the Chimú kingdom (dotted area). The area round Lima is known as the central coast, that around Moche as the north coast and that around Nazca as the south coast.

1
The land and the people

The Andes form the backbone of the western South American republics. From barren foothills, a few kilometres from the shore, they rise steeply to over 6500 metres (21,000 feet). Numerous short rivers flow westwards from the continental divide, providing fertile oases for human habitation amidst the stony desert of the coast. To the east of the divide are the longer north-flowing tributaries of the Amazon, wending their way through lofty plateaux and high valleys. Altitude influences climate and modifies the effect of being close to the equator, creating greater diurnal differences in temperature than seasonal ones, all of which determine the kind of crops that can be grown. Potatoes are important at high altitudes, up to 4000 metres (13,000 feet) above sea level. Lower down, around 2000 metres (6500 feet), come maize, squash and beans, and in the warmer valleys the sweet potato, peanuts, cotton and tropical fruits. Stock rearing has always been important in the highlands; huge flocks of llamas and alpacas once roamed the tableland around Lake Titicaca. These have dwindled in many areas to be replaced by sheep, and llamas are rarely used as beasts of burden, as they were in precolumbian times.

The grandeur of coastal and highland scenery can obscure the real hardships for those who live there. The Andean peasant of both zones has always been dependent on water in the right amount and at the right time. If the winter rains are late or sparse, there will be insufficient water in the irrigation ditches and crops can fail. Too much rain may cause mudslides and the burial of an entire village. Some soils are fertile enough to yield two harvests a year with irrigation, but many Indians are forced to live on the poorer, marginal soils.

The prehistory
People entered the New World across the Bering Strait, then a land bridge from Siberia, towards the end of the last ice age. The most reliable radiocarbon dates for their presence in the central Andes range from 14,000 to 12,000 BC, by which time they were living in small bands in rock shelters like Guitarrero Cave in north Peru. They lived by hunting deer, camelids and small rodents and by gathering roots and berries. By 6000 BC temporary fishing camps had been established on the coast and by

2500 BC there were permanent villages at Huaca Prieta, Ancón and Asia. Their inhabitants cultivated squash, beans and chile peppers and supplemented their diet with fish and shellfish. Pottery was unknown, although textile production was well established, but based entirely upon cotton and bast fibres. Gradually settlements expanded into coastal valleys, which were uncultivable without some form of irrigation. By 1800 BC there were ceremonial centres in both coast and highlands and pottery appears as a well developed craft, which was probably introduced from elsewhere.

From then on features that are peculiarly Andean develop: ceremonial centres consisting of massive platform mounds or an intricate labyrinth of rooms, agriculture based on intensive cultivation and storage of maize and the potato, animal husbandry based on camelids, highly developed metallurgy in gold, silver and copper, ancestor worship, a system of corvée labour and the keeping of records by means of knotted strings known as *quipus*. Projecting backwards from Spanish chronicles, we can deduce that most villages had a chief who was often subordinate to a more powerful one elsewhere. Some villages held land,

2. Llamas roped together and resting near Puno, Peru. The llama and its close relative, the alpaca, are domesticated camelids. Their pelts come in a variety of colours ranging from white to shades of brown and black. Domestication encouraged the breeding of white animals since their wool can be dyed in more colours.

fishing or grazing rights in other areas. For example, a village near Lake Titicaca might hold lands higher up, suitable only for grazing, some around the lake for growing potatoes and some in a warmer valley for growing maize and avocados. At the same time certain coastal peoples engaged in active trade, bartering salt and fish for highland products such as wool, metals and turquoise.

Other aspects of Andean society are the preoccupation with life after death, seen in the burial of the dead either in tombs constructed in their own houses or in special ritual chambers. The bodies were accompanied by abundant grave goods, such as textiles, pottery and food, which were renewed periodically. The dead were venerated for a long time and consulted by their living relatives on various matters. On certain festivals important

4. A wooden doll from Nazca, probably a talisman. It is wrapped in plain-weave wool cloth dyed by the *plangi* method in red, dark blue, dark green, gold and white. Probably late Middle Horizon. Height 25.5 cm (10 inches). (Courtesy of the Liverpool Museum, National Museums and Galleries on Merseyside.)

deceased ancestors were dressed in new clothes and paraded around the locality, a custom that survives in the dressing of local saints' statues in indigenous clothing and parading them around the village. On their arrival in Cuzco, the Spaniards were horrified to find retainers fanning one of the long-dead Inca emperors, dressed in all his finery and seated on a stool. The local shaman was also important. He or she held special status in each village and gave advice on future events, potential enemies and successful harvests. Sometimes the shaman spoke on behalf of a *huaca* or sacred object, which could be an unusually shaped rock, a dead ancestor or a particularly large maize cob. These *huacas* were worshipped and received offerings of cloth, which were buried or burnt. Some of them gained more than local fame and were believed to foretell the future. Pachacámac, near Lima, is one example, for pilgrims from all over Peru flocked there regularly to pay homage at his shrine.

The Incas were one of several tribes struggling for power in the Cuzco area. By the mid fifteenth century, through a combination of superior warfare, skilled diplomacy and luck, they were able to gain the hegemony of the region from Lake Titicaca north to Abancay. They seem to have been led by men of organisational and military genius: firstly Pachacuti; then his son Topa Inca, who conquered the powerful coastal Chimú kingdom; then Pachacuti's grandson, Huayna Capac, who extended the territory to Ecuador. The heirs of the last-named emperor, Atahualpa and Huáscar, were quarrelling over the succession when the Spaniards arrived in 1532. Francisco Pizarro, leading only about a hundred men, was able to take advantage of this quarrel and the divided loyalties of the various subject tribes and swiftly made himself master of Peru.

The Colonial and Republican Periods

For some thirty years after the conquest Peru was torn apart by quarrels between the conquistadors themselves. During this period the coastal population declined by two-thirds, partly owing to civil strife, partly through newly introduced European diseases and partly because of the ill-treatment of the Indians by their new masters, who forced them to work in the mines, treated them as beasts of burden, tore down their shrines, burnt their ancestors' bodies and expropriated their lands. By 1565 the succession of viceroys appointed by the Spanish Crown was fully in control and most indigenous rebellion had been suppressed. The dispersed Indian population was concentrated into European-style towns and villages laid out on a grid pattern. Administratively most of the old Inca Tawantinsuyu became the Viceroyalty of Peru (the word Peru arising from a Spanish misunderstanding about the name of the country) until the battle of Ayacucho in 1824, when Simón Bolívar and republican forces assured the final independence of the Spanish-American colonies. The land was subsequently divided into two countries, Peru and Bolivia. During the last century of Spanish rule there were rebellions on the part of the Indians, culminating in the revolt of Tupac Amaru in the 1780s. However, this rebellion was crushed and the Indians played little part in the wars of independence.

Liberation from Spain did not improve their lot. A form of tribute was still exacted from them until the end of the nineteenth century. Moreover, the rise of large coastal estates dedicated to the growing of cash crops for export created a labour force of wage-earning peasants working land they did not own. In the highlands land can be owned by individuals or communities, who share it out between their members, each receiving according to

5. A family from Charazani, Bolivia. The husband wears a knitted cap under his felt hat and a plain poncho. The wife wears a traditional headband under her hat and warp-patterned carrying cloths over her shoulders. (Courtesy of J. Hill and Dover Publications.)

his needs. However, crop yields can be low since the best land has been expropriated by wealthy Creoles. Furthermore, as plots are divided up for inheritance, land shortage has driven many to seek work in coastal cities.

The modern Quechua and Aymara

Contemporary Andean Indians are generally divided into two groups according to the language they speak, either Quechua or Aymara. Both languages are similar in structure and may have sprung from a common parent some thousands of years ago. Quechua, the language of the Incas, is spoken in the highlands of modern Peru and Ecuador and was imposed by the Incas in certain regions of Bolivia. Aymara is generally spoken in Bolivia and parts of northern Chile. In modern Peru it is spoken in some areas east and west of Lake Titicaca. It was once more extensively spoken, particularly in the centre and south of Peru, but was displaced by Quechua several hundreds of years before the Inca conquest.

There are many similarities between the cultures of the people speaking these languages. Both groups use indigenous looms to make textiles for themselves and for tourists. For themselves they weave clothes, blankets, carrying cloths, sacks and saddlebags. For the tourist they weave belts, ponchos, bags and coverings and knit a variety of garments. Knitting with two needles is a recent development, for this technique was unknown to the pre-columbian Indians. Instead most textiles were loom-woven and can be divided into two kinds: warp-patterned weaves and weft-patterned weaves. The former survived throughout the Colonial Period and form the basis for decorative ponchos and carrying cloths manufactured in the highlands today. The latter found their highest expression in the tapestries woven through much of Peruvian prehistory, and which did not last through the eighteenth century. Some precolumbian techniques, such as warp ikat, have survived only sporadically, while others, such as gauze weaves and painted cloth, have disappeared from the repertoire.

2
Materials and tools

Peruvian peasants have always used the simplest of tools. The spinning and weaving equipment found in precolumbian graves closely resembles what is still in use today. Canes, both solid and hollow, served as loom bars and heddle sticks; loom posts and weaving swords were made from the wood of local trees, as were some of the larger shuttles. Needles for sewing and darning came from cactus spines or were made of copper. Small combs of wooden prongs bound with cotton were used to beat down the weft, and the warps were picked up with bone tools made from camelid metatarsals. After the Spanish conquest, some new materials and tools were introduced, such as sheep's wool, silk, linen, the treadle loom and the spinning wheel. In the nineteenth century came aniline dyes and, in the twentieth, synthetic fibres. All of these, however, have merely been incorporated into the time-honoured methods of cloth production, and perhaps only in the case of aniline dyes can the new be said to have superseded the old.

Methods of processing animal and vegetable fibres can differ slightly from region to region, so that there are exceptions to the following general account which summarises ancient and modern practices.

Spinning

The major fibres of precolumbian Peru were cotton and camelid wool. The cotton, *Gossypium barbadense*, is thought to have been introduced as a primitive domesticate into northern Peru from southern Ecuador some time in the fourth millennium BC. It is a hardy plant, more resistant to drought than modern hybrid strains, and has longer fibres. It occurs naturally in six colours: white, grey, tan, medium brown, reddish brown and dark brown. Nowadays its cultivation and processing are confined to the north coast of Peru around Mórrope, but in precolumbian times it was grown as far south as northern Chile.

According to James Vreeland, indigenous cotton can be harvested continuously for up to six years after planting. The seeds are removed from the bolls by hand and the resultant wads of cotton are beaten with sticks until the fibres are evenly distributed. They are then folded and rolled into a cylinder which is attached to a vertical post or a wooden tripod. The spinner sits on the ground nearby with her spindle across her thigh. With her

6. North coast cotton spinners still use the ancient tripod to which they attach the beaten fibres. This woman from Mórrope holds the spindle horizontally across her thigh and draws out the fibres with her left hand while rotating the spindle with her right hand. (Courtesy of the Vreeland/Sican Archive.)

left hand she draws the fibres from the bottom of the cylinder, twisting them and rotating the spindle with her right hand. As a sufficient length of thread is formed, it is wound around the spindle, which requires no whorl. Representations of spinning on precolumbian coastal pottery show that a similar method was used then. Chronicles also state that the spindle was twirled in a small bowl resting on the ground. Such bowls are often found in the baskets of weaving tools that accompany mummies.

Wool, with its longer fibres that give greater friction when rubbed against each other, can more easily be spun by the drop-spindle method. The chief sources of wool for the ancient Peruvians were the two domesticated camelids, the llama and the alpaca. Llama wool is coarser and greasier than alpaca wool and is consequently used for heavy-duty articles, such as mats, sacks, saddlebags and cordage. The alpaca is a smaller, shaggier animal, with softer, longer hairs, although the coarsest alpaca wool will intergrade with the finest llama wool. Another wild member of the same family, the vicuña, has even finer hairs which were much prized by the Incas. According to the chronicles, these animals were captured during special hunts and sheared. No commoner under the Incas was allowed to wear vicuña wool cloth, this being a privilege reserved for the emperor and the nobility. Today the vicuña is a protected animal and the manufacture of garments from its hair is forbidden.

Alpacas are sheared between December and March. Their wool is spun by women and young girls as they go about their daily chores. It is not usually carded. Instead the fibres are pulled out by hand and arranged parallel to one another to form a roving. This may be wound around the forearm or on to a forked wooden distaff. The spindle is a smooth stick with a wooden whorl. The spinner makes a small length of yarn by twisting together some fibres with her fingers. She attaches this to the spindle, which she twirls and drops, while drawing out the fibres from roving with the thumb and forefinger of her other hand. As the yarn is spun, it is wound on to the spindle. Sheep's wool is prepared and spun in a similar way. A few communities in the central highlands use the spinning wheel, but its disadvantage is that the spinner has to stay in the same place all the time and cannot engage in other activities.

Some of the earliest textiles in the Andes come from the hard fibres, chiefly from *Furcraea occidentalis*, a cactus plant that resembles the agave, with narrow, sharp-pointed leaves that can yield fibres up to 50 cm (20 inches) long. Other plants were also

7. Highland women spinning wool with a drop spindle. Their black skirts with a red border, warp-patterned shawls and flat pancake hats are typical of the Cuzco region. The two boys wear brown, warp-striped ponchos over European-style trousers and sandals of tyre rubber. (Photograph: Rosalie Gotch.)

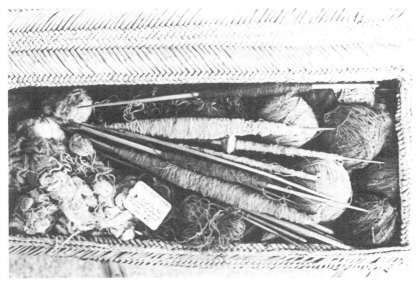

8. The interior of a reed workbasket with balls of yarn, spindles and raw cotton. Such workbaskets are common in coastal graves. In the centre of one spindle is a small bead, often called a spindle whorl, but its probable function was to prevent the thread from slipping off the spindle. Spindle length about 22 cm (8½ inches). (Courtesy of the Pitt Rivers Museum, Oxford.)

utilised, including a bast from a kind of milkweed, *Asclepias* species. The leaves or stems were probably soaked for a long period and then beaten to release the fibres, which were spun by being rolled between the palm of the hand and the thigh, a procedure known all over South America. In preceramic times the bast was plied with cotton, but it was used on its own in fabrics made from a single element, such as looped pouches and fishing nets.

During spinning, fibres may be twisted either to the left or to the right, resulting in spirals that resemble either the letter Z or the letter S. Single yarns are usually plied together with a heavier spindle, in order to make a stronger, more even thread, and this ply is nearly always done in the opposite direction to the initial twist. The direction of spin and ply have varied over time and place and can be important in identifying the provenance of certain textiles. Wool, both then and now, is almost always Z-spun and S-plied. The direction of the spin of cotton varies. In the highlands today woollen yarns spun with an S twist are called *lloq'e* and deemed to have magical properties. They may be spun only on special occasions, such as for cloth offered to Pacha-

9. A woman from Ferreñafe on the north coast of Peru weaving a cotton saddlebag on a backstrap loom. The shuttle lies on the ground to her left. She grasps the heddle stick with her left hand and the shed rod with her right. The weaving sword is inserted in front of these, just behind the piece already woven. The precolumbian north coast preference for warp-striped fabrics with paired warps and wefts still prevails among these artisan weavers of native cotton. (Courtesy of the Vreeland/Sican Archive.)

mama, the earth goddess, and as a protection against sickness. Travellers wear *lloq'e*-spun yarns around their wrists as a talisman against harm on a journey.

Dyeing

Cotton was dyed before spinning and wool after spinning. A variety of dyes was used and a number of different hues obtained: as many as 190 have been counted in the ancient textiles from Paracas and Nazca. Wool takes colour better than cotton, which could be dyed only in shades of blue, red and brown. Most dyes came from local plants. For example, the *molle*, *chilca* and *taro* trees of coastal valleys gave shades of yellow; blue came from the indigo plant and red from a madder-like plant known as *relbunium*. Purple could be obtained from the secretions of a shellfish and another red came from the cochineal beetle, which lives on the prickly pear cactus. Colour was also affected by the mordants used, the most common of which were alum and urine. There was also an iron-based one, which has often rotted the yarns.

The dyeing processes of antiquity probably resembled modern ones. One method from Bolivia is to soak the wool in both hot and cold water and then dry it, in order to eliminate any air pockets which could cause uneven colour saturation. Water is then brought to the boil in an earthenware pot and the mordant, usually a powdered alum, is mixed in until it has dissolved. Next the crushed dye plants are added and the mixture stirred and left to boil for several hours until the desired colour is obtained. At this point the wool is immersed in the dye and simmered for half an hour. The pot is removed from the fire and the wool is left to soak overnight. The next day it is taken from the bath, rinsed in clear water and dried in the sun. The procedure varies slightly according to the kind of vegetable dyes and the mordants used.

Weaving
The backstrap loom is considered to be typical of the Andes, although other types have been used since antiquity. Its popularity stems from the fact that it is simple to make and can be easily dismantled and transported. Nowadays narrow warp-patterned belts and straps are woven on it, but it can be used for the wider webs of ponchos and mantles. Its disadvantage lies in the fact that the breadth and sometimes the length of the web are restricted by the nature of the loom, for it would be extremely tiring to weave anything wider than the span of one's arms, and therefore the maximum width of the web is about 75 cm (30 inches).

To set up the loom, the warps are usually wound around two posts in a figure of eight. Each post is then replaced by a heavy cord which is lashed to a loom bar. One loom bar is attached to a vertical post or to a peg on the wall. The other loom bar is attached to a belt which passes around the weaver's waist. By leaning backwards or forwards the weaver can adjust the tension of the warps as he or she desires. One shed is formed by the winding of the warps in the figure of eight, the other by picking up the alternate warps, that is those in the lower layer of the first shed, with small loops of cotton known as leashes, and attaching them to a heddle stick. Pulling the stick upwards brings the lower layer of warps to the top and creates a second shed. In order to weave elaborate patterns other sheds can be created by picking up the warps with a bone tool or by making more leashes.

For some time archaeologists were puzzled as to how the very wide webs of some precolumbian shirts were woven. These can measure as much as 250 cm (98 inches) wide and would have been most easily woven on some kind of vertical loom. The chronicles had reported their existence, but there was no archaeological evidence for any until 1958, when excavations at Pachacámac revealed a blackware vessel with a vertical loom modelled on its top. The loom consists of two upright posts connected by an upper cross-beam, from which the warps hang. Such a loom has also been reported ethnographically from among some southern communities. It too consists of two upright posts with a cross-beam set across the forked ends and another beam lashed to the base. It is set up in an outside courtyard close to a wall and the whole is wide enough for two weavers to sit comfortably side by side.

Another kind of loom found today in the highlands is the four-stake, horizontal ground loom. This consists of four small posts wedged into the earth with the loom bars lashed to them about 25 cm (10 inches) from the ground surface. As with the vertical loom, its tension is fixed from the start but can be

10. Guaman Poma, a seventeenth-century chronicler, depicts an elderly Indian man working at a vertical loom. He is using a bone pick to separate groups of warps. The Spanish caption reads: 'In the villages of this kingdom the friars are so bad-tempered and so strict that they beat the Indians to make them work and there is no escape for them.'

11. (Left) A woman from the Potolo region of Bolivia, weaving a poncho on a horizontal ground loom. She is using a bone tool to pick up the warps needed for the pattern. To her right is a long shuttle. (Courtesy of J. Hill and Dover Publications.)

12. (Right) A man from the Potolo region of Bolivia, drawing out the warps on a treadle loom to be attached to a post behind him, in preparation for weaving *bayeta* cloth. (Courtesy of J. Hill and Dover Publications.)

modified by the addition or subtraction of extra weaving swords and shed sticks. It is particularly used for warp-patterned weaves among the Aymara. No direct archaeological evidence exists for the use of this loom in antiquity, but it was probably known along with the other two types.

The Spaniards introduced a fourth type, the treadle loom, which was used in textile workshops during the Colonial Period. It was worked chiefly by men, as it is today in the highlands, where a coarse woollen cloth known as *bayeta* is woven on it. *Bayeta* is warm and hard-wearing and peasants make plain skirts, trousers and jackets from it.

Most weaving probably took place in the exterior courtyards of dwellings, as it does today on all types of loom mentioned. In the three indigenous looms, the warps are not attached to the loom

bars, but to a thick cord which is lashed to the bar. Thus they do
not have to be cut in order to remove the finished cloth from the
loom: the result is a four-selvedge fabric. On the backstrap and
horizontal looms weaving begins at one end with the insertion of
a thicker weft for two or three shots. These wefts are known as
heading cords or loomstrings and they set the width of the web.
The weaving progresses for several centimetres of plain or
patterned cloth, at which point it is abandoned. The opposite end
is then begun in the same manner and continued until the part
already woven is reached. The last few shots of weft have to be
made with a darning needle, since the shed is too small to allow
the passage of a large shuttle. In the case of warp-patterned
weaves such a procedure leads to patterning irregularities known
as the terminal area. This can be spotted in both ancient and
modern textiles, since it is always a few centimetres away from
one of the end selvedges.

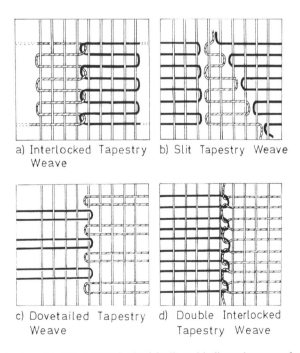

a) Interlocked Tapestry   b) Slit Tapestry Weave
   Weave

c) Dovetailed Tapestry   d) Double Interlocked
   Weave   Tapestry Weave

13. Diagram to show the different methods of dealing with discontinuous wefts in tapestry
weave.

3
Techniques

Woven cloth consists of two sets of elements: warps (the longitudinal yarns) and wefts (which interlace the warps, usually at right angles). In ancient Peru the majority of textiles were in plain weave, either of one colour or with a simple stripe, check or plaid design. Plain weave refers to a structure whereby the first shot or passage of the weft passes over and under one or more warps and the following shot reverses the procedure, that is those warps that lie above the weft in one row will lie below it in the next. Most of these surviving plain-weave specimens come from the coast and are made of cotton. Some are woven in a balanced-count weave, with the warp and weft given equal prominence, that is the same number of warps and wefts per centimetre. The majority, however, are warp-faced, where the warps outnumber the wefts, usually covering them entirely, so that the latter appear as faint horizontal ridges. As a variation, one can find the warps paired, the wefts paired, or both warps and wefts paired. The Chimú weavers favoured paired, single-ply warps and other areas experimented with one or the other during the very early periods.

Tapestry

Tapestry is considered to be a weft-faced weave executed in a variety of colours to form some design. In addition, the wefts are discontinuous, that is they turn back along their path at certain points in order to create blocks of colour or outlines in accordance with the needs of the design. The warps are completely covered by the wefts and appear as faint vertical ridges. Although tapestry is commonly executed with wool wefts on cotton warps, examples of all-cotton tapestry are known, particularly for the earlier periods when wool was not widely available over all the coast. Some highland tapestries are entirely of wool, such as those tunics and mantles from Tiahuanaco that are found in northern Chile.

There are several techniques for dealing with the boundaries between wefts of different colours. Sometimes these boundaries appear as long slits, when each weft is turned back around its marginal warp along the direction in which it came. These slits can form part of the design if, for example, there is a stepped pattern. However, very long slits weaken the structure of the

14. Slit-weave tapestry in red, gold and green wool on cotton warps. The slits enhance the diagonal lines of the pattern, but the longer ones have been sewn up. Total fragment is 29 by 15 cm (11 by 6 inches). (Courtesy of the Trustees of the Victoria and Albert Museum.)

15. Reinforced tapestry in which red, blue, yellow and black wool wefts are woven over cotton warps with extra cotton wefts to strengthen the fabric. South coast. Middle Horizon. Total fragment is 130 by 63 cm (51 by 25 inches). (Courtesy of the Pitt Rivers Museum, Oxford.)

cloth and were wholly or partially sewn up after weaving. One method of retaining the sharp outlines of slit-weave tapestry is to reinforce the cloth by a finer weft which runs through the total width of the fabric at intervals, so that for every two wool wefts there would be an invisible one of fine cotton. Different coloured shapes in slit-weave tapestry can be outlined in a contrasting colour with wefts that do not run perpendicular to the warp. These are known as eccentric wefts because of their oblique or curved passage, and they too may help to strengthen slit-weave tapestry. Otherwise, wefts of different colours can be linked during their passage. This linking can take place between warps, when it is known as interlocking, a technique that is characteristic of highland tapestries. Double interlocking occurs when one weft passage links two wefts of the adjacent colour, forming a ridge on the wrong side of the fabric. This technique is relatively rare in Peruvian tapestries but found on the south coast during earlier periods. A further method is dovetailing, when wefts of different colours turn around a single warp, which they can do singly, in pairs, or in threes to give a toothed effect.

In precolumbian and modern Peru the ends of the different colours were finished off by being invisibly darned into their corresponding colour area, so that both faces have an equally well finished appearance. In the past, however, wefts were sometimes floated across the back of the tapestry to the next area where they were to be used, giving a right and a wrong side to the fabric. This was a common practice on the south coast during the Late Intermediate Period.

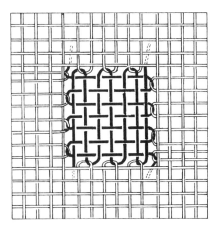

16. Diagram to show the structure of discontinuous warps and wefts. Here the two colours are joined by interlocking, but other methods, such as dovetailing, could be used instead.

Discontinuous warps and wefts

One unusual technique is where the warps as well as the wefts are discontinuous. This occurs on fabrics that appear to have a kind of patchwork design, although the whole web was woven as one on the loom. The pieces are usually in a balanced-count plain weave and must have been woven on some kind of frame loom. The main warps were set up as usual from one loom bar to the other. They were crossed at intervals by a series of wefts known as scaffold wefts, which were normally of a finer yarn than the wefts of the fabric. These scaffold wefts would have been held taut by being fastened to the sides of the frame loom. From them hung other shorter warps for the length required for their part in the design. They were interlocked with adjacent upper and lower warps of different colours. The cloth was then woven, with the weft colour varying according to the warp colour and interlocking with wefts of adjoining sections. After the fabric was completed, the scaffold wefts were withdrawn. The American Museum of Natural History in New York possesses a small loom which demonstrates this warp set-up, with the scaffold wefts still in place.

Supplementary warps and wefts

A common technique in ancient and modern Peru is to create a design by floating extra warps or wefts over the ground weave. If this is done without disturbing the basic structure of the weave, the additional warps or wefts are known as supple-

17. Tunic in plain-weave cotton in shades of brown and white with a yellow wool fringe. The design is created by means of discontinuous warps and wefts and shows long-billed sea birds whose heads are orientated vertically within a step fret pattern. North coast. Late Intermediate Period. 47 by 131 cm (18½ by 51½ inches). (Courtesy of the Textile Museum, Washington DC.)

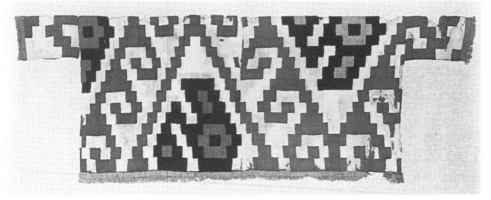

18. The two faces of a small cloth with supplementary warp and weft floats forming a design of stepped crosses. Blue and white cotton. Central coast. Late Intermediate Period/Late Horizon. 45 by 25 cm (17½ by 10 inches). (Courtesy of the Trustees of the Victoria and Albert Museum.)

mentary. The background is either a balanced-count or a warp-faced plain weave. If the pattern is made by means of supplementary warps, these occur at regular intervals and follow the general order of interlacement of the background cloth, but on occasions they float over it to form the pattern. Supplementary warps are continuous throughout the weave and are placed in position during warping. On the other hand, supplementary wefts can be continuous or discontinuous. If the former, they can be floated along the back of the cloth when not required, giving an obvious right and wrong side to the fabric; or else they can create the same design in the negative on the reverse of the cloth. If discontinuous, they are usually inserted along with the passage of the main weft for part of the way and

Peruvian Textiles

19. Detail of fish brocaded by means of dis-
c o n t i n u o u s s u p-
plementary wefts in
blue and white cotton
and brown wool on
white plain-weave cot-
ton. Probably central
coast. Late Intermedi-
ate Period. (Courtesy
of the Birmingham
Museum and Art Gal-
lery.)

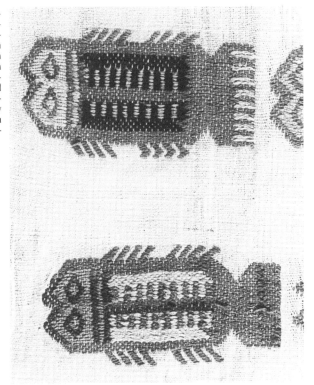

are worked backwards and forwards until the design is achieved.
If this technique is carried out on the loom, it is called
brocading. If it is done off the loom and the needle pierces the
yarns of the weave, it is best considered embroidery.

Complementary warps and wefts
A more elaborate technique for producing warp-faced
patterns is one whereby warps of two different colours are set up
in two complementary sets that are both necessary to the
structure of the fabric. In other words, there is no background
cloth against which the design is created. Instead, each warp has
its counterpart on the opposite face of the cloth and the design
springs from the interlacement of the weft with these two sets.
For example, as the weft passes over a warp of one colour, it
must pass under its reciprocal warp of the other colour. Thus a
design is created with the colours in reverse on each face and the
fabric is double-faced. If each set of warps is coequal in this

20. A backstrap loom from the north coast of Peru. Probably Late Intermediate Period. Double cloth is being woven in brown and white cotton with a design of cats and step frets. The cloth is lashed to the loom bars by cords that pass through the loom strings. Two heddle sticks and one shed rod can be seen in the warps. Size of the textile is 25 by 20 cm (10 by 8 inches). (Courtesy of the Trustees of the British Museum.)

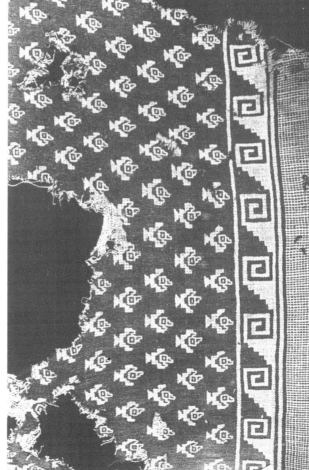

21. Brown and white cotton double cloth with a design of sea birds and a step fret border. The two surfaces can be seen where the brown has frayed. The reversal of the motif along diagonal lines is an important feature of ancient textiles. Central coast. Late Intermediate Period. Warps are horizontal. 21 by 33 cm (8½ by 13 inches). (Courtesy of the Cambridge University Museum of Archaeology and Anthropology.)

manner, they are known as complementary warps. The same kind of structure can be found on weft-faced fabrics with reciprocal sets of wefts. Complementary-warp weave has always been a popular method of creating designs in the highlands, where patterned warp stripes are interspersed with plain warp stripes on various garments (figures 30 and 32). In antiquity complementary-weft weave was popular on the coast as a border for tunics or mantles.

Double cloth

Double cloth has a long history going back to the Early Horizon. Two separate layers of warps are required. These are set up on the same loom, one on top of the other, each with its own heddle stick and shed rod. Each layer is of a different colour and has its own weft of the same colour. Two webs are woven in a balanced plain weave and the design is formed by the warps and wefts of one colour crossing from one layer to the other, thereby interconnecting the webs at certain points. When the cloth is removed from the loom, one can feel the two webs and the sections where they interconnect. A variation of this technique is known as tubular weaving and has been used to produce strong bag and girth straps. Again there are two layers of warps set up to produce a warp-faced cloth, but the weft is single and spirals round from one surface to the other so that the resultant cloth would be a tube but for the fact that the warps are interchanged between layers and warp colours not needed for the pattern are left floating between the two layers of the fabric. Such a technique is also found on the warp-patterned stripes of certain Bolivian ponchos and mantles.

Gauze weaves

Gauze refers not to a light, filmy material, but to the kind of weave used to produce a slightly openwork fabric, where the warps are crossed at regular intervals and eventually return to their original position, each crossing being secured by the passage of the weft. A simple crossing of left over right warps, in pairs, will give such an openwork effect, however heavy the yarn. There are more complicated sets of crossings by which intricate patterns may be woven. Gauzes were normally made of white cotton or fine wool and were further embellished with embroidery or tapestry.

A technique sometimes confused with gauze is that of openwork, where warps and wefts are deliberately omitted or bunched together so that the fabric looks like a mesh, with

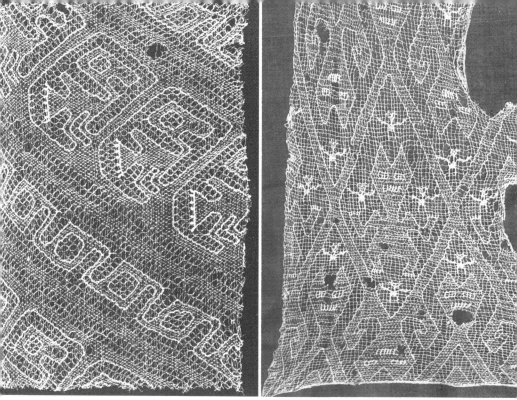

22. (Left) Gauze weave combined with embroidery in cream cotton to give a design of sea birds along diagonal lines. Central coast. Late Intermediate Period. Warps are horizontal. 26.5 by 39.5 cm (10½ by 15½ inches). (Courtesy of the Birmingham Museum and Art Gallery.)

23. (Right) Openwork fabric of white cotton with rectangular and triangular spaces ornamented with embroidery. The design shows monster men with the major figures reversed along vertical lines. Probably central coast. Late Intermediate Period. 23 by 18 cm (9 by 7 inches). (Courtesy of the Liverpool Museum, National Museums and Galleries on Merseyside.)

square, diamond or triangular spaces. Usually the spaced wefts are knotted with half hitches around the spaced warps to make a stronger fabric and to keep the spacing even. Designs of cats or birds were often embroidered on this background. The best examples are from the central coast and were made in fine white cotton.

Embroidery

Embroidery has been used in different ways throughout Peruvian textile history: a maximum effect was achieved with a minimum of stitches. In the Early Horizon it was a major means of creating elaborate designs, but by the later periods it was used merely to finish a garment. The best known embroideries are those from graves in the Paracas peninsula; these were executed in a counted stem stitch, with the needle going over four threads and under two. When the thread is kept to the same side of the

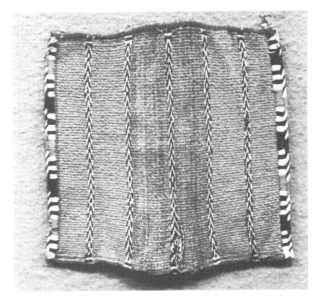

24. Coca bag in warp-faced plain weave with warp stripes and a chevron design in yellow, black and red wool. There is buttonhole-stitch edging in the same colours. Central coast. Late Horizon. 17 by 16 cm (6½ by 6 inches). (Courtesy of the Trustees of the Victoria and Albert Museum.)

needle all the time, the effect is one of a twill weave. As a variation, however, the rows of stitching can be counterpaired, with the thread kept above the needle on one row and below it on the next, which gives a different texture to the cloth. A double running stitch was also used to create designs, particularly during the Inca period, when it was used zigzag to finish the bottom of a tunic, which was further bound in buttonhole stitch, as were the edges of Inca bags.

Possibly the most interesting of the precolumbian stitches is the cross-knit loop stitch, which resembles crossed knitting on two needles in a stocking-stitch manner. However, it was made on a single needle by taking the loop around the crossing of the loop of the previous row. It can be executed vertically or horizontally on the fabric itself to form an embroidered area, used as a tubular edging to garments or worked into a fabric in its own right. Outstanding examples are the mantle borders of birds, flowers and agricultural deities worked in multicoloured wool in this stitch and dating from the Early Intermediate Period (figure 36). To form the body of the figures, a small hank of vegetable fibres was used as a support and the design was built up in rows of stitches around it.

Twining

Before the invention of the heddle loom, twining a pair of wefts around fixed warps would have been as quick a method of cloth manufacture as darning the weft over and under each warp. In this case the warps were not set up in a figure of eight because no shed control was needed. Instead they were wound around fixed loom bars in a cylindrical fashion. They were probably turned around a horizontal cord set midway between the bars, each loop placed in the opposite direction to the previous one, so that when

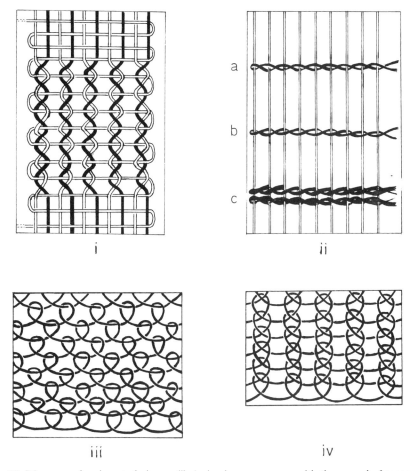

25. Diagrams of various techniques. (i) A simple gauze weave with the second of every pair of warps crossed over the first and held down by the weft. (ii) Weft twining: (a) twining in a Z direction; (b) twining in an S direction; (c) the two kinds paired to give a chain-stitch effect. (iii) Simple loop stitch. (iv) Cross-knit loop stitch.

the cloth was finished the cord could be pulled out, leaving a four-selvedge fabric. Twining started at one side of the warps from the centre point of a doubled weft, which would be interlaced with the warps in an S or Z manner, that is crossing the right end of the weft over the left end, or vice versa. Patterns were made by colouring the warps or wefts, crossing the warps in different directions, counterpairing the wefts or changing the spacing of warps and wefts.

Painting

The painting of cloth goes back to the Preceramic Period, when certain pigments were rubbed on to the warps or the finished cloth. By the Early Horizon designs were painted on plain-weave cotton fabrics, probably with small animal-hair brushes. Pigments were limited to browns, greys, reds, blacks and an occasional blue or purple. They were probably made from ground minerals mixed with water and some resinous substance to make the paint adhere better. Designs were first outlined in black and then filled in with colours. By the later periods some repetitive motifs seem to have been stamped on the cloth by using a carved gourd as the stamp.

26. Painted cloth of warp-faced, plain-weave, brownish cotton. The design represents amphibian-like creatures and birds painted in a greenish brown pigment. 34 by 22 cm (13½ by 8½ inches). Central coast. Late Intermediate Period. (Courtesy of the Manchester Museum.)

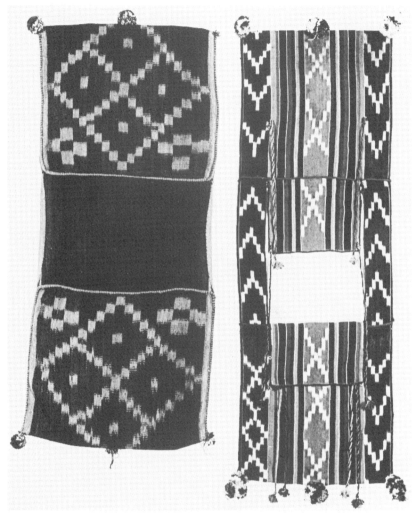

27. Two saddlebags with a simple geometrical design in warp ikat. White, black and red sheep's wool. Tarabuco, Bolivia. Twentieth century. 94 by 40 and 102 by 36 cm (37 by 15½ and 40 by 14 inches). (Courtesy of J. Hill and Dover Publications.)

These late painted cloths have an overall pattern of fishes, birds and local coastal deities. The technique continued into the Colonial Period, from which a few altar cloths with Christian religious scenes painted on them survive.

Tie-dyeing

Forms of tie-dyeing go back to the Early Horizon, but neither the ikat nor the *plangi* method was well developed in Peru. Warp ikat was used to make geometrical designs, mostly variations of stepped crosses. In this technique, which is found on warp-faced textiles, the warps are dyed in the required design before weaving commences. Certain portions of the warp are tightly bound to prevent them from taking colour when the skeins are immersed in the dye bath. Patterns can be made in several colours, provided that the lighter colours are dyed before the darker ones. Nowadays the technique is found on saddlebags, ponchos and shawls from various Andean countries.

The *plangi* method is used to dye designs on cloth that has already been woven (figure 4). Again the portions of the design to be left in reserve were tightly bound so that they did not become saturated with the dye. This technique was used for patchwork-type cloths from the central and south coasts. Small patches were woven by the discontinuous warp and weft method described previously. They were disassembled and each piece dyed in a different colour combination, usually in reds, greens, purples and blues. The separate pieces were then reassembled on the loom. The designs were mainly small circles arranged in a lozenge.

Other techniques

Cloth can also be made from a single element or yarn that is worked into itself like modern crochet. Mention has been made of cross-knit loop-stitch borders. Pouches, hats and bags were also made by this technique, as well as by simple and knotted looping. The latter technique was used for all kinds of nets. Braiding with a set of yarns, where any one can play the part of warp or weft, was elaborated to produce slings and headbands, usually with a lozenge or chevron design. Sprang, or the interlinking of a set of elements, was used for hoods, caps and small bags.

There were many techniques for embellishing cloth, one of which gives a pile surface. Such a surface is found on small squarish hats and on animal figures worked in tapestry-weave. The hats are worked in loop stitch with square knots set close together. In every other row along the sides of the hat an extra weft was caught into the knots to form a small loop, which was later cut to give a plush effect. In the tapestry-weave animal figures loops were made between each warp by the weft during its

28. Pile cap with corner tassels. The sides and crown are worked in a brown wool loop stitch and the sides are embellished with pile tufts of red, green, blue, yellow and black wool. Designs are based on Tiahuanaco iconography. Probably south coast. Middle Horizon. Height 8 cm (3½ inches). (Courtesy of the Birmingham Museum and Art Gallery.)

passage from one side of the web to the other. The looping was repeated every row, or every other row, as required, and left a furred surface whose loops were often left uncut.

A garment or wall hanging could be sewn with ornaments such as tassels, pompons or spangles of perforated metal, shell, bone or stone, which sometimes completely covered the original. Today in Charazani, Bolivia, small beads are threaded to the weft at the end of one shot and before the beginning of the next to give a beaded border to belts and straps. The feathers of tropical forest birds made a spectacular adornment. They were attached to the cloth in rows by bending the ends of the quills over a thread and fastening them down with another thread which was knotted around the bend in each feather. The threads were stitched down to the fabric so that the rows of feathers overlapped. Designs of animals and deities were worked out in different colours for tabard-like garments and high-crowned hats (figure 49).

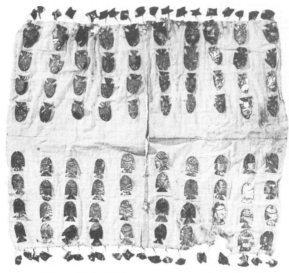

29. Small tabard, possibly a child's. Plain-weave cream cotton with yellow metal spangles shaped like fish and bells. The fish are reversed at the shoulder line. Probably north coast. Late Intermediate Period. 38 by 51 cm (15 by 20 inches). (Courtesy of the Manchester Museum.)

30. Detail of a garment border in red and cream wool with white cotton wefts just visible. The sea-bird design is woven in a complementary-warp weave (the warps are horizontal) and the separately woven red wool fringe has been sewn to the border with a neat hemming stitch. Band width is 5 cm (2 inches). Central coast. Late Intermediate Period. (Courtesy of the Trustees of the Victoria and Albert Museum.)

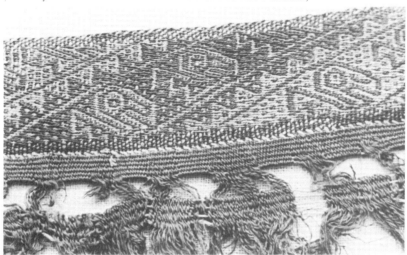

One of the most popular finishes for all periods has been the fringe, which is often made separately from the main fabric and attached by an overhand stitch. Warps were set up for the desired length of the fringe and a few shots of weft were inserted. The warps were then removed from the loom and the free ends left to twist or they were cut. Sometimes groups of warps were given an S or Z twist to provide a thicker fringe. More elaborate fringes were made from small tabs which could be worked in tapestry, cross-knit loop stitch or buttonhole stitch.

Some well used garment fragments have been patched and darned. Such darning can be crude, with no attempt made to match up colours or threads, which is surprising in view of the Peruvians' advanced weaving skills. Either fine objects came into the hands of those who could not sew well and they were unable to mend them properly, or else sewing skills were not prized in antiquity. Nowadays a torn piece may be rewoven rather than darned or patched, much like our invisible mending.

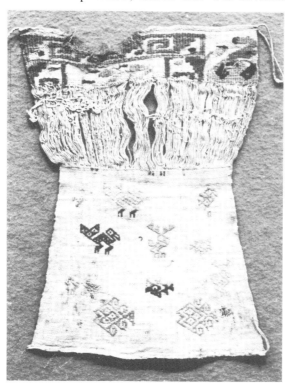

31. Samplers have always been used for practising techniques, designs and their layout. This one has been deliberately shaped inwards by increasing the weft tension. The thicker heading cords can be seen at both ends. Fish, cat and bird motifs have been brocaded on the lower half with discontinuous supplementary wefts. Above the loose warps the brocading resembles tapestry. Red, blue, gold and beige wool on white cotton. Central coast. Late Intermediate Period. 37 by 29 cm (14½ by 11 inches). (Courtesy of the Trustees of the Victoria and Albert Museum.)

4
The characteristics of Peruvian textiles

Certain recognisable characteristics set Peruvian cloth apart from other indigenous weaving traditions. In the first place, fabrics were not tailored. They left the loom in a rectangular shape and two or more webs were sewn together to make a garment. Warp selvedges are indicated by the heading cords; weft selvedges are plain and only rarely reinforced by bunching the final warps together or by pairing them.

In precolumbian Peru, however, a few garments were roughly shaped on the loom. This was done by increasing and then decreasing the weft tension, which resulted in the hourglass shape of some breechcloths. To make a piece wider, new warps could be added as the weaving progressed; to make it narrower, existing warps could be paired and then cut, as in the case of certain bags which were narrower at the top than the bottom.

The terminal area has already been mentioned. On finely woven cloth it may be difficult to discern, so carefully have the last few shots of weft been inserted with the needle. On modern textiles this area stands out because the patterning in the warp stripes becomes fuzzy. Some weavers maintain that this is done so as not to produce a perfect piece of cloth, with the implication that this would offend their deities. In a modern shawl or carrying cloth the two webs are reversed when sewn together, so that one terminal area is at the bottom and the other at the top.

Usually three webs 40-60 cm (16-24 inches) wide were needed for an ancient mantle and two webs for a tunic. These webs were sewn together with a simple overhand stitch or occasionally with a figure-of-eight stitch. For a patterned garment identical webs had to be woven and some forethought given to the matching of the motifs. Sometimes these do not exactly match each other in the finished garment, which suggests that the size and spacing of the motifs were worked out by eye rather than by counting each warp and weft.

For a tunic two webs were stitched together along the weft edges, leaving a centre gap for the neck. The sides were sewn to a convenient distance from the shoulder in order to leave room for the arms. Some tunics were given sleeves, which were small rectangles folded in two and inserted into the armholes. Bags were made from a single piece of cloth that was folded in half and sewn up the sides.

An important feature of both ancient and modern textiles is the

32. A coca bag made from a carrying cloth or shawl. Warp-faced plain weave with two warp-patterned areas. The outer two stripes in each triad are in complementary-warp weave and the inner stripe is in supplementary-warp weave. The strap has been woven at a later date and is in supplementary-warp weave with both faces visible on the right. The terminal area can be seen in the centre. Black, white, red and pink sheep's wool. Bolivia. Twentieth century. 31 by 33 cm (12 by 13 inches).

use of several techniques on a single garment. The main pattern may be achieved by supplementary wefts with some embroidery. A border of tapestry weave or complementary-weft weave may be added and the edge bound with cross-knit loop stitch to which fringes, tassels or pompons are attached. In some pieces the wefts can become warps, which can be subsequently woven in a different pattern. Furthermore, similar designs can be rendered in a variety of techniques. For example, some of the figures in this book show the same stylised sea bird executed in tapestry weave, discontinuous warps and wefts, gauze, complementary-warp weave and double cloth.

At the same time, certain motifs recur throughout Peruvian textile history. From the Preceramic Period onwards there is abundant use of geometrical designs such as step frets, volutes, S and Z shapes. Humans and animals have always been popular: in antiquity these were cats, fish, birds and snakes; nowadays, they tend to be horses, bulls and llamas. Overall patterns of a single repeated motif were usually executed with supplementary wefts or in double cloth. A pictorial effect could be created with tapestry or painting, but the result was usually a symmetrical composition.

For webs needed for tunics the design was sometimes woven in reverse when the shoulder line was reached, so that it did not appear upside down on the back of the wearer. Otherwise motifs were reversed along diagonal or vertical lines, or interlocked from opposing angles. In this way part of the design was always visible to an onlooker from the right way up.

In the ancient textiles colours tended towards the darker hues of their range and often contrasted vividly with one another. In the Paracas embroideries as many as eighteen colours can be found on a single mantle and each small figure can show from nine to thirteen colours. In these early periods, the combination of reds and blues is striking; in the late periods, the golds, greens, rose-pinks and browns harmonise well in certain tapestries. In the modern textiles the occasional juxtaposition of bright colours, such as magenta and green, can be jarring. To offset these clashes narrow toning stripes are placed between contrasting colours to provide a transition between them.

33. Fragment of cloth in slit-weave tapestry. As viewed, with the warps horizontal, it depicts diagonal rows of sea birds. If it is rotated 90 degrees so that the warps are vertical the birds become stylised cats. Red, gold, green and white wool wefts on cotton warps. Central coast. Late Intermediate Period. 35 by 12 cm (14 by 5 inches). (Courtesy of the Trustees of the Victoria and Albert Museum.)

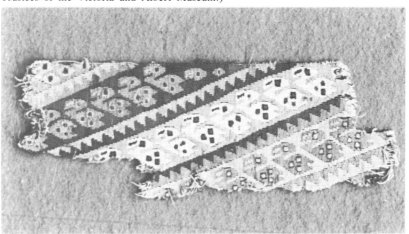

5
The development of Peruvian weaving

Preceramic Period, 12,000-2000 BC

The earliest textiles, dating from 8600 BC, were found in 1969 in excavations at Guitarrero Cave in the north highlands of Peru. Fibres from *Tillandsia*, a bromeliad, *Furcraea*, a kind of agave, and some grasses were interlinked, twined and looped to make baskets and pouches. These early fragments may not be true cloth, but they document the first tentative steps towards cloth production, which probably had its origins in twined basketry.

By the beginning of the third millennium BC the inhabitants of coastal fishing villages were making twined textiles, sometimes plying one cotton single yarn with one bast single yarn, probably because cotton cultivation was still in its infancy. Designs were made by crossing the warps and depicted condors, snakes, crabs and human figures. Some woven cloth is also found in plain weave, with warp stripes or with designs made by floating the warps over a plain weave background. Colour variation was obtained by contrasting the natural colours of the cotton or by rubbing a red pigment over the yarns. A few yarns were dyed blue. These early twined textiles are in a fragmentary condition and were probably burial wrappings.

Initial Period and Early Horizon, 2000-400 BC

The invention of the heddle stick to raise the second shed meant that weaving was no longer a laborious task akin to modern darning, but an efficient method of cloth production. This invention took place at the beginning of the Initial Period and led to the demise of twining. However, techniques like looping and sprang continued to be used for bags, pouches, hats and turbans. There was considerable experimentation with the yarns used. On the north coast cotton was consistently S-spun and, instead of being plied, two single yarns were used for the warp and sometimes for the weft. On the south coast warps and wefts were eventually S-spun and Z-plied. On the central coast both Z-spun and S-spun yarns were used.

The earliest tapestry comes from the central coast and dates to the Early Horizon. It is all cotton and depicts a condor head with wefts dovetailed around a common warp. It is during this period that wool became available in greater quantities on the south coast, but not on the central or north coasts. A few wool yarns

34. Detail of a preceramic twined textile from Huaca Prieta in the Chicama valley, Peru. The warps are paired and the twining is in a Z direction. (Courtesy of the American Museum of Natural History, New York.)

have been found as decoration on the weft selvedge of cotton textiles from the preceramic site of Aspero, but there is no sustained use of wool on the central and north coasts until the Early Intermediate Period. It is likely that camelids were first domesticated around Lake Titicaca in the south highlands, and therefore it is logical that wool should appear earlier on the south coast than elsewhere. Unfortunately, we know nothing of the early development of wool textiles in the highlands but there must have been a strong tradition of spinning, weaving and dyeing there by the beginning of the Early Horizon.

All techniques of fabric construction known to the ancient Peruvians were in existence by the end of this period. These include double cloth, triple cloth (where there are three interconnected layers of fabric), discontinuous warps and wefts, some early wool tapestry and warp wrapping, where the design is created on the warps before weaving by wrapping them in coloured yarns. The earliest painted textiles are from Carhua, south of Paracas. The cotton cloth is painted with representations of deities from Chavín de Huántar, with fanged mouths, snake appendages and eyes with crescent-shaped pupils. The most spectacular cloth, however, comes from graves excavated in the Paracas peninsula in the 1920s by the Peruvian archaeologist Julio César Tello. These graves contain bodies seated in baskets and wrapped in several large shrouds to form a bundle. Interspersed with the shrouds are sets of embroidered garments and articles of personal adornment. The embroideries, which are worked in wool on cotton cloth, depict mythical monsters or shamans wearing animal masks and clutching a sacrificial knife in one hand and in the other a trophy head (a human head severed from its torso). Early Paracas embroideries were executed in a style which emphasises the angularity of the figures. Later embroideries utilise more colours and resemble the creatures found on Nazca pottery. Their makers were the first to use wool extensively and to realise its potential for creating designs.

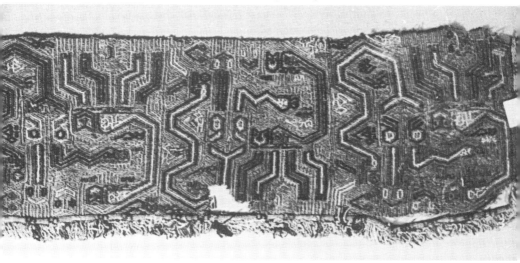

35. Detail of two garment borders from Paracas. Wool stem-stitch embroidery on a plain-weave background with a cross-knit loop-stitch border and a fringe. Above is a feline monster in dark blue, green and yellow on a red background. Below are double-headed intertwined serpents in red, green, yellow and brown on a blue background. South coast. Early Horizon to Early Intermediate Period. (Courtesy of the Bolton Museum and Art Gallery.)

Early Intermediate Period and Middle Horizon, 400 BC-AD 900
These periods saw the rise of tapestry weave executed in wool wefts on cotton warps as the chief means of creating patterns on coastal textiles. As wool became more plentiful on the central and north coasts it was used for more and more of the textile. Tapestry is an effective way of using up small lengths of wool, which could be dyed in a wider range of colours than cotton and so enhanced the pictorial qualities of the fabric. On the south coast tapestry borders were made for the neck slits and armholes of tunics. Designs were geometrical or depicted mythical animals in blues, yellows and pinks with a black outline. There were long fringes to garments and cross-knit loop-stitch borders became very elaborate. Embroidery lost its pre-eminence and deities formerly embroidered in stem stitch were now painted on cotton cloth.

On the central and north coasts cotton tapestry continued alongside wool tapestry until well into the Early Intermediate Period. Various kinds of tapestry weave occur, although the slit method eventually became dominant. Popular designs were double- or multiple-headed snakes, fish and fish deities, super-

36. Detail of a cross-knit loop-stitch mantle border showing birds pecking at flowers, in red, blue, yellow, green and pink wool. South coast. Early Intermediate Period. (Courtesy of the Birmingham Museum and Art Gallery.)

37. Details of a garment fragment in tapestry weave with interlocking joins and some dovetailing. The design motifs are based on Tiahuanaco iconography. The garment would have been worn with the warps horizontal. Black, gold, red, white and pink wool. Provenance unknown. Middle Horizon. (Courtesy of the Cambridge University Museum of Archaeology and Anthropology.)

natural beings and geometrical motifs, particularly the interlocking step fret.

At the beginning of the Middle Horizon a new style reached the coast of Peru. It can be traced to the site of Tiahuanaco in Bolivia and is thought to have reached coastal Peru via the site of Wari in the central highlands. This style is found on pottery, tunics and hangings that reproduce the motifs of Tiahuanaco, such as the central figure on the Gate of the Sun, attendant winged messengers, pumas and condors. These tunics differ from coastal ones, for the warps lie horizontally across the chest of the wearer, rather than vertically, and the two webs were sewn together down the warp edges. Some tunics found in northern Chile, and thought to be from the actual site of Tiahuanaco, were woven in one piece, with the neck slit achieved by making the warps discontinuous. These hangings and tunics were made in interlocking tapestry weave rather than the slit-weave tapestry of the coast. Their colours are vivid shades of red, gold, brown, blue and black. Motifs are elongated and compressed and sometimes elements of the typical Tiahuanaco face are split up and

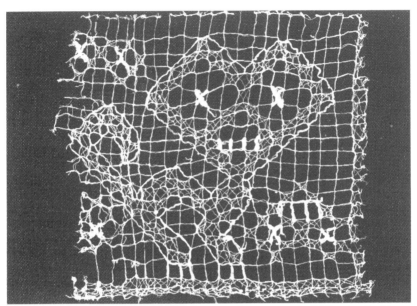

38. Openwork fabric in white cotton with rectangular spaces and additional embroidery, which depicts a cat. Central coast. Late Intermediate Period. 17 by 18 cm (6½ by 7 inches). (Courtesy of the Birmingham Museum and Art Gallery.)

recombined in small rectangles. By the end of this period these motifs were being painted on to cotton cloth.

Late Intermediate Period and Late Horizon, AD 900-1532

Much of the cloth in Western collections comes from these periods. Tapestry was still important and on the coast slit-weave tapestry regained its prominence, depicting birds, fish, cats, interlocking snakes and dignitaries or deities with elaborate head-dresses. Overall designs tended to be achieved with brocading via supplementary wefts. On the central coast around Chancay gauze weaves and double cloth became popular. On the north coast rich geometrical patterns in brocaded double cloth gave way to tapestry showing small men with crescent head-dresses surrounded by monstrous birds with trophy heads. Chimú weavers specialised in sewing feathers, gold and silver spangles, beads and tassels to their garments.

The Inca conquest brought changes leading to a certain standardisation of cloth production, probably because of the creation of textile workshops manned by specialist weavers. Tapestry was still the most valued technique. The finest tapestry was known as *qompi* cloth and the coarser plain weave used for peasant clothing and everyday articles was known as *awasca*. Tunics from Inca graves are of several recognisable types. Like the earlier Middle Horizon ones, they were woven in interlocking tapestry weave with the warps running horizontally across the chest and were usually woven in one piece. On both bags and tunics motifs are geometrical and very neatly executed.

Colonial and Republican Periods, AD 1532 to present

The Spaniards were quick to realise the importance of textiles to the Indians and lost little time in turning this fact to their own advantage. Textile workshops known as *obrajes* were set up to weave various kinds of cloth for the new Creole population. Some of the former Inca textile workshops continued to weave tapestry hangings that incorporated birds, animals, flowers and Spanish coats of arms. However, by the end of the eighteenth century such hangings were no longer fashionable and tapestry weaving had virtually died out. In the *obrajes*, *bayeta* was woven with sheep's wool on the newly introduced treadle loom. In the meantime Indians continued to produce warp-patterned weaves

39. Fragment of cloth in plain weave with tapestry-weave bands for which the warps are paired. This piece, with its typical Inca design of stepped crosses, shows the high technical standards of the period. Red, yellow, white and brown wool on a dark blue wool background. Provenance unknown. Late Horizon. 18 by 28 cm (7 by 11 inches). (Courtesy of the Birmingham Museum and Art Gallery.)

for their own clothing, both ceremonial and everyday. The better pieces, destined for festive occasions, were handed down from generation to generation.

Nowadays patterning on cloth is still achieved via complementary- or supplementary-warp weaves, with warp-faced double cloth popular in Bolivia. Braids for slings continue to be made and such finishing devices as embroidery, fringes and tassels are still in use. With the introduction of aniline dyes, colours have become very bright with particular emphasis on shades of red and magenta. Often the motifs are worked out in white or black against a coloured ground. Stripes prevail rather than overall patterns, because they suit the nature of warp-faced textiles. The motifs incorporated within these stripes consist of human and animal figures, some grossly distorted, others fantastic. Geometrical designs are also found, most of which hark back to the precolumbian periods, for example volutes, small hexagons, crosses, triangles, diamonds and S shapes. However, the bindings on the edges of shawls, bags and ponchos are now woven in a float weave with lozenge or chevron motifs rather than made in cross-knit loop stitch.

40. Tapestry hanging woven after the Spanish conquest. It may have covered the back of a choir seat. Various coloured wool wefts with a red background weft on cotton warps. The curvilinear designs and the central bishop's symbols reveal Spanish influence. Provenance unknown. Colonial Period. 62 by 53 cm (24½ by 21 inches). (Courtesy of the Trustees of the Victoria and Albert Museum.)

6
Dress ancient and modern

Precolumbian dress

The Spanish chronicles give us detailed descriptions of Inca clothing, but for the earlier periods we have to rely on archaeological evidence in the form of the textiles themselves and of sculpture and ceramics that depict garments worn by both sexes. The most complete textiles come from burials, both looted and scientifically excavated. Although some of these garments were made especially for the dead (because they show signs of being unfinished or their proportions make them unwearable), certain tunics must have been worn, as demonstrated by dirt marks around the neck and armholes. Occasionally tunics seem to have been remade from other pieces. Furthermore articles could be 'killed' before being placed in a mummy bundle. Breechcloths were tied in one corner and hangings were deliberately torn before being buried as an offering. At the same time the fact that one finds both fine and coarse clothing patched and darned shows how much even the simplest article was valued. The emperor Atahualpa's garments were carefully kept and annually burnt so that no one could get hold of a piece and use it to cast an evil spell upon him.

From Paracas on the south coast and the Chimú kingdom on the north coast we find matching sets of male garments with the same design appearing on a loincloth, mantle, tunic and turban. The Paracas burials contain several such sets. A complete costume consisted of a loincloth, wrap-around skirt attached by ties, sleeveless tunic, small poncho, a headband or turban and a large mantle worn draped over the shoulders. No footwear has been found in these burials, although presumably people wore some kind of sandal like those of later periods. The mantles, which averaged 275 by 130 cm (108 by 51 inches), were usually of plain-weave cotton or cotton and wool and embroidered with rows of figures. The same figures could be repeated on the borders which ran along both lengths of the mantle and turned part of the way along each width to form two diagonally opposed L shapes that never meet. These figures could also be repeated on the border of other garments. The tunics were sleeveless but short and wide so that they covered the upper portion of the arm like a cap sleeve. They were usually given elaborate fringes around the armholes. For the headband, feathers were attached

FIESTA DELOS CONDESVIOS
AIAMILLAZAIИATA

FIESTA DE LOS COLLASVIOS
HAИSCAMAIICO.CAB
CA·COLLA·

ABRIL
CAMAI·IIИCAPAIMI

COREOИ
HATVИCHASQVI·

41. Different forms of indigenous dress, as portrayed by the chronicler Guaman Poma: (top left) south coast dancers with elaborate feather tunics and head-dresses; (top right) south highlands men with fez-like caps and women with peaked hoods; (bottom left) the Inca emperor and his queen at the festival of Capac Raymi in April; (bottom right) a colonial messenger wearing a precolumbian tunic over Spanish breeches.

42. How the garments from the Paracas burials might have looked when worn by a man from that period: (left) in a tunic, kilt and headband; (right) in a tunic, loincloth, mantle and headband. (Courtesy of Anne Paul.)

to a braided strip of cloth which was wound around the head. Turbans were rectangular pieces of cloth which were placed on the head so that they hung down the side or the back.

Although over a thousand years separate the two cultures, similar matching sets have been found in Chimú graves. The loincloths were larger, 338 by 114 cm (153 by 45 inches) as opposed to 100 by 50 cm (39 by 20 inches) for Paracas ones. They had ties at one end which secured the cloth around the wearer's waist, leaving the decorated front panel to fall down in front of the wearer like a skirt. The tunic was also wide and short, but with sleeves. Turbans were worn like Paracas ones but secured by wimple-like bands wrapped around the head and chin. There were also large mantles, as much as 329 by 190 cm (130 by 75 inches) in size. These garments often matched in design and colour schemes. Judging from ceramic representations, women were dressed in long tunics with small cloaks. They went

43. Headband from a matching set of garments in plainweave white cotton with supplementary-weft brocading in brown and grey cotton and black wool, with a black wool fringe. The overall design is one of stepped triangles and zigzags. North coast. Late Intermediate Period. 437 by 17 cm (172 by 6½ inches). (Courtesy of the Department of Library Services; negative 325451 by Yourow. American Museum of Natural History, New York.)

44. Loincloth that matches the previous headband. Shown folded. Without ties 367 by 106.5 cm (144½ by 42 inches). (Courtesy of the Department of Library Services; negative 325454 by Yourow. American Museum of Natural History, New York.)

45. Mantle that matches the previous headband and loincloth. Shown folded. 170 by 142 cm (67 by 56 inches). (Courtesy of the Department of Library Services; negative 325453 by Yourow. American Museum of Natural History, New York.)

bareheaded or brought their cloaks up to cover their heads.

Inca clothes from the highlands were slightly different. A common man wore a small, plain loincloth and a tunic, an *uncu*, that was sleeveless and longer than coastal tunics, so that it reached to his knees. It was plain or striped. Over it he wore a mantle, which he knotted over his shoulder to leave the arms free for working. The mantle could also be used for sitting on or carrying objects, as it is today. Surviving Inca tapestry tunics were probably worn by nobles or government officials. They range from 84 to 100 cm (33 to 39 inches) long and 72 to 79 cm (28 to 31 inches) wide. They were patterned in rows of rectangular geometrical designs known as *tok'apu* or else had chequer-board patterns in black and white with a V-shaped red border around the neck. Sometimes there were just two bands of *tok'apu* around the waist. The Inca emperor and nobles wore knee and ankle fringes, bracelets and necklaces, and in their pierced ears were huge circular earrings which pulled down their ear-lobes. Ordinary men wore a small headband around their head, but the Inca emperor had a special band with several little red tassels encased in gold tubes, which fell over his forehead from a central head-dress ornament.

A woman wore a tunic known as an *aksu*, made from a single piece of cloth wound around her body, with the two ends brought over her shoulder from behind and fastened with pins called *tupu*. These were made of gold, silver or copper and had large, flattened heads. Over her shoulders she wore a mantle known as a *yacolla* and a patterned belt, a *chumpi*, was wound around her waist. Highland women wore a band called a *wincha* around their heads. Over this noblewomen placed a folded cloth.

Both sexes wore sandals on their feet. The soles were made of untanned llama or deer skins, or else from plaited vegetable

46. (Left) A woman from the Potolo region of Bolivia wearing an overskirt that is pinned over her shoulders. It is in warp-faced plain weave with a design of monster birds in complementary-warp weave in red, black and white sheep's wool. (Courtesy of J. Hill and Dover Publications.)

47. (Right) A woman from Tarabuco, Bolivia, wearing traditional dress that consists of an overskirt with a complementary-warp weave patterned border, a shawl with warp stripes, fastened by a pin, and a leather cap. (Courtesy of J. Hill and Dover Publications.)

fibres, with thongs of braided wool or cotton. The nobility carried small bags, *chuspa*, containing coca leaves.

Colonial dress

During the early part of this period the Indian peasant retained his dress and head-dress as a mark of his race. The one change demanded by the Spanish church was that women sew up the slit in their wrap-around tunics, since their thighs were sometimes visible as they walked, which offended the Spanish clerics. Local chieftains and the remaining Inca nobility who wanted to curry favour with the Spaniards soon adopted Spanish dress, reserving their native attire for festive occasions. The lower down the social scale, the fewer the items of Spanish clothing that were worn. Most Indian men kept their sleeveless tunic and mantle but would add breeches, boots or shoes, a high-crowned hat and sometimes a ruff.

Towards the end of the eighteenth century the Indian rebellions, although crushed by the Spanish authorities, resulted in a clamp-down on any manifestation of Indianness. This led to the strict enforcement of some earlier laws banning Indian clothing. Men were obliged to replace tunic and mantle by a shirt and trousers, and women their long tunic by a skirt and blouse. The only indigenous items retained were an occasional headband, belt and small cloak or shawl for the women. The men adopted the poncho instead of the mantle. This garment was probably developed by the Araucanian Indians of Chile as a protection when riding horses in bad weather. Although there were a few poncho-type garments in ancient Peru, they were much smaller than the modern version, which is ubiquitous in the Andes and no longer confined to Indians. It is usually made in plain stripes of brown and fawn for everyday wear and in brighter colours for festive occasions. European-style felt hats were introduced soon after the Spanish conquest and were quickly adopted by the Indians, with the result that their manufacture became an indigenous occupation.

Modern dress

In general the Quechua and Aymara are similarly attired and can be differentiated only by their hats and the woven patterns on their clothes. In the wealthier communities men wear European-style factory-made suits and in the poorer ones trousers and round-necked shirts of *bayeta*. In certain parts of the south highlands the trousers have fancy woven bands around their bottoms. In the Cuzco area trousers are black and reach to just below the knee. In some areas of Bolivia and Ecuador they are white. Over these a man wears a *bayeta* jacket and a poncho and may use another square cloth, a *lliclla,* for carrying things. Some men still carry a small bag for coca leaves. Sandals are now made from old car tyres because of their hard-wearing properties. For festive occasions men may wear a wide belt around their waist. On Taquile Island, in Lake Titicaca, these belts have designs that symbolise the agricultural year. In many regions men wear a felt trilby-type hat or a panama. On the high plateau, near Lake Titicaca, they wear a knitted cap with ear flaps, a *chuyllo,* under the hat. In Cuzco for festivals one sees men wearing a low-crowned, flat-brimmed hat trimmed with braids and tassels, which is known as a *montera.*

Women's apparel also varies in colour and head-dress from region to region. Around Cuzco a plain, dark *bayeta* skirt with a narrow patterned band around the hem is worn with several wool petticoats. On the head is a *montera,* similar to the men's. Around Lake Titicaca Aymara women wear a pleated skirt or one with horizontal tucks in bright colours. Bowler hats are common there. Everywhere the *bayeta* blouse is gradually being replaced by one of synthetic fabric and a cardigan. The only items woven on an indigenous loom will be a headband or *wincha* (now only worn by women from Charazani in Bolivia), a belt, a shawl for carrying babies and a *lliclla* for carrying other objects. Small bags are hung from the belt and larger ones slung over the shoulder. In Tarabuco, Bolivia, women wear a variation of the old *aksu* as a wrap-around overskirt which is pulled over the shoulder and belted. Both sexes there wear a strange helmet, similar to a Spanish conquistador's leather helmet.

7
Textiles and society

In many pre-industrial societies textile production is considered a woman's occupation, but in Peru men have always carried out some of the tasks associated with it. The chronicles indicate a varied division of labour in spinning and weaving. Figure 48 shows a woman spinning and a man plying, but this may have been true only of peasant yarn production. The women who lived secluded in convents under the Incas probably undertook both skills and produced the fine yarns to be woven for tapestry. Nowadays women still do most of the spinning, although some men are equally capable and will do it if required. Small boys near Cuzco will help prepare fleeces and men will help with the plying. On the north coast of Peru it is common for men to do the plying for yarns destined for cordage. On Taquile Island men spin and knit.

We have less historical information on dyeing. One chronicler, Falcón, mentions male specialist dyers who served the Inca emperor, but it was probably chiefly a woman's task. In present-day Bolivia dyeing is done by women, but the pictures and descriptions of colonial *obrajes* show that men dyed mass-produced cloth. They earned a Spanish *real* a day (a mere pittance in modern terms) for dyeing two pieces of cloth, each 100 metres (about 330 feet) long.

With regard to weaving, the Jesuit priest Father Cobo reported that there were male specialists in tapestry weaving who lived in small colonies and wove *qompi* cloth for the Incas. The person working on the vertical loom, depicted by Guaman Poma (figure 10), is probably an elderly man. A vessel from Pachacámac shows a male overseer and two women weaving. Nowadays in southern Peru large pile tapestry rugs and hangings are woven on a vertical loom by men, whereas women in the same village use a small backstrap loom, on which they make everyday clothing. In the highlands men have always worked the treadle loom, and in certain regions they also use the backstrap loom, on which they weave ponchos, saddlebags and shawls. Many of the pieces woven for tourists today are made by men and men have traditionally made braids for slings and cordage.

With regard to the time factor in cloth production, recent studies suggest that hand-spinning the necessary amount of yarn can be more time-consuming than the weaving process. Reports on spinning in the Cuzco area show that 10-13 metres (33-43 feet) of yarn can be spun in ten minutes by experienced spinners. An elaborately patterned poncho can take up to 508 hours to make, that is almost four months of work, if one works a 35 hour week, with the time almost equally divided between spinning the yarn and weaving. On the other hand, a plainer poncho, with a few simple warp stripes, takes only 288 hours to make, but 200 of these are spent spinning yarn. In the central highlands it can take a man between two and five days to weave such a poncho. These facts have led people who want to earn money by making goods for tourists to use machine-spun yarns and synthetic fibres, the cost of which is not much more than that of a high-quality sheep's fleece. Because of the long time taken to spin yarn, people concentrate on weaving small objects, like belts and bags, for these do not require so much yarn or labour investment, since it may be difficult for women or men, burdened by domestic and agricultural tasks, to find time to weave a poncho.

We can use these modern studies to calculate the amount of labour involved in spinning and weaving some of the ancient burial garments. For example, James Vreeland has calculated that 65 km (almost 40 miles) of yarn were required to weave the wrappings of a Late Intermediate Period mummy bale, whose total length exceeded 60 metres (197 feet). The estimated spinning time for this yarn was 4442 hours: in other words, one woman working a 35 hour week would take two and a half years to complete the spinning alone. For the embroidered Paracas garments it has been estimated that it would take one person working a 35 hour week more than ten years to produce the cloth for one bundle. All this attests to the considerable amount of time spent by the populace in producing cloth for the dead, not taking into account clothes for the living, textile offerings to deities and tribute to local chieftains.

Spinning takes place at odd moments throughout the year. Weaving, however, tends to be done in the slack agricultural season between July and November, that is between harvesting and planting, remembering that the weaver works outside and is dependent on daylight and dry weather. People learn how to spin, dye and weave through observation and imitation of those already in possession of such skills, usually a close relative. A four- or five-year-old girl will be given some fleece and a spindle and will be expected to work out the details in solitude, while tending a flock of animals on a hillside. These young girls, not yet old enough to engage in heavier household tasks or to weave, have the time to produce a good deal of yarn. Weaving is a skill

48. (Below) Guaman Poma depicts a man and woman outside their house. The woman is spinning from a distaff held in her left hand. The man is plying from two yarns wound into a ball on to a larger spindle.

49. (Above right) Feather head-dress with black and white feathers applied on to brown network. From forehead to feather tip it measures 41 cm (16 inches). The piece hanging down at the back is of red, black and white feathers and is 40 cm (15¾ inches) long. North coast, Late Intermediate Period. (Courtesy of the Cambridge University Museum of Archaeology and Anthropology.)

similarly learnt from one's mother at the age of ten or twelve. At that time a mother will give her daughter a small bag or carrying cloth to weave and will help her to warp it. She will assist her with working out the warp pattern, correct her errors and help her with difficult sections like the terminal area.

Both in the past and today textiles have more socio-cultural meaning than is commonly realised. Mention has been made of how they indicate people's origin and status. Similarities in the size and design of certain Inca tunics suggest that they were woven to specifications laid down by the emperor and worn as a badge of office. For instance, Atahualpa's escorts at Cajamarca are described as wearing red and white chequer-board tunics. Only the Inca emperor was allowed to wear garments sewn with gold and silver ornaments and he alone could present these as gifts to his subordinates. In precolumbian Peru one's head-dress revealed one's place of origin, something the Spaniards found useful for census purposes. Nowadays in Tarabuco, Bolivia, people can easily identify the village someone comes from by the patterns woven on their clothes.

Textiles were also given as gifts at certain ceremonies, much as we might give money. In ancient Peru they were presented to the participants in various rites of passage, such as when a child was first named or had his hair first cut. At initiation ceremonies for Inca nobles boys received a breechcloth specially woven for the occasion by their mothers. On marriage the bride gave the groom a fine wool tunic and a headband. Nowadays such gifts are made by the sponsors of the ceremony, usually the most important uncle. These customs survive in Bolivia, where a woman weaves a set of traditional clothing for herself, plus blankets and storage sacks, before marriage. All this is considered part of her dowry and, if the couple should part, the textiles return with the woman. It is a woman's skill as a weaver that makes her a desirable partner, for in the first year of marriage she is expected to weave a poncho for her husband and later a set of clothing.

The importance of textiles is also emphasised by the amount demanded in tribute, first by the Incas and then by the Spaniards. In the Chillón valley during the Late Horizon one group of villages was obliged to give the Incas 117 male tunics and an equal number of female tunics, plus 26 pieces of *qompi* cloth. At Pachacámac in 1549 the Indians still had to provide their Spanish overlords with fifty shirts every quarter year. Before the conquest the Inca state controlled a good deal of cloth production and distribution, for theoretically it owned all the herds of llamas and alpacas and had also set aside fields for cotton cultivation. The raw cotton from these fields and the camelid fleeces were distributed among villages, where they were spun and woven into garments, shirts, sacks and carrying cloths. When finished, these articles were taken to state warehouses in the highlands, where they were redistributed as gifts to those who had won the emperor's favour, to the army or to peasants doing labour service at state centres, for all these were fed and clothed by the Inca state. Chroniclers of the Spanish conquest report the Spaniards' amazement at the number of warehouses filled with cloth, which retreating Inca armies would burn rather than let fall into Spanish

50. Modern festive attire worn by *mestizos* from a central highland village. The women wear imitation Indian clothing consisting of a brightly coloured dress with metal spangles sewn on the bodice, a shawl that has been machine-embroidered with a floral design, *broderie anglaise* petticoats, white panama hats and high-heeled shoes. The men are masked and have pink and green feathers attached to their hats.

hands. Cloth was also exported, for during Pizarro's first voyage to South American shores he met a Peruvian raft bound for Ecuador, carrying cloth to exchange for spondylus shells and emeralds.

Ritual bundles of cloth play an important role in animal fertility ceremonies, when herds of alpacas, llamas and sheep are blessed and sometimes marked. The bundles consist of specially woven carrying cloths with warp-patterned stripes, which contain smaller cloths, coca bags, animal figurines, foodstuffs and shells. The bundle is opened in the animal corral during the ceremony, the cloth is spread out and offerings of coca and alcohol are made to local deities. At the end of the ceremony the bundle is carefully wrapped up, returned home and hidden away until the following year.

In modern Andean society indigenous clothing affirms the Indians' identification with their own culture, as opposed to the European culture of their conquerors. Those who wish to be classified as non-Indians first change their dress, and women their hairstyle. With the growth of national consciousness fostered by military and other governments since the late 1960s the Indian has theoretically been accorded greater status, so that *mestizos* (those of mixed Indian and Hispanic ancestry who follow an urban lifestyle) are adopting a version of Indian dress for their festivals. Such a costume symbolises their identification with the Indian part of their heritage, without their having to dress like Indians.

As a development from the kind of garments woven for themselves, Indians are now producing weavings for tourists. It is possible to purchase the plainer striped ponchos worn by the men, and the occasional festival one, but more common are those knitted from loosely spun alpaca wool or hand-woven from synthetic fibres. Spinning the yarn for these goods is not so time-consuming for knitting yarn does not have to be so fine and evenly spun as yarn for weaving. Hence a variety of socks, sweaters, mittens and caps are made for the tourist market. The patterns show llamas, humans, star shapes and other geometrical motifs in the natural browns, blacks and white of alpaca wool. The art of dyeing with vegetable dyes is being revived and wool is being dyed in soft colours; tapestries are being woven from it, sometimes on a treadle loom. The warps are synthetic yarns or cotton and the wool weft is thicker than any precolumbian yarn used for tapestry, so that the surface is rough. These tapestries depict geometrical motifs that are set diagonally or in rectangles and are loosely based on Inca or Tiahuanaco designs. The joins are dovetailed rather than interlocked. Some very coarse tapestries with precolumbian motifs are also being woven with an exceptionally thick sheep's wool weft. A different style has been evolved at San Pedro de Cajas, where tapestry-like pictures are woven with a coloured unspun wool weft which is pushed in between fine warps to create a picture that portrays an idealised version of Indian life. These woven pictures are intended as wall hangings.

One may dislike some of this weaving, which does not approach the standard by which Indians weave their own ponchos and mantles, let alone precolumbian standards, but there is no denying that textile production for tourists is becoming a vital part of Indian economy. In the late 1960s, Junius Bird, the doyen of Peruvian textile analysts, wrote that spinning and weaving were becoming a dying art, as machine-made fabrics took their toll of homespun and woven ones. He suggested that those who are in a position to do so would be well advised to encourage the highest standards of craftsmanship and see that the craftsman or woman receives adequate returns for his or her labour. If he or she does not receive this encouragement, then Peruvian weaving will be but a pale reflection of past glories.

51. A modern tapestry woven for tourists. Synthetic warps and sheep's wool wefts in beige and brown with some yarns dyed with natural vegetable dyes. The designs are loosely based on Middle Horizons ones. Compare figure 37. Provenance Cuzco, but possibly made elsewhere; twentieth century. 95 by 63 cm (37 by 25 inches).

8
Museums

Many museums in Britain have collections of Peruvian textiles. However, few will put their collections on permanent display because prolonged exposure in display cases can lead to rapid deterioration of textiles, even in a controlled museum environment. Those museums with good collections will rotate some examples; others will display them only for special exhibitions. Bearing this in mind, the intending visitor should make careful inquiries in order to avoid disappointment. The museums marked with an asterisk usually have some Peruvian items on display.

United Kingdom
Birmingham Museum and Art Gallery, Chamberlain Square, Birmingham B3 3DH. Telephone: 021-235 2834.
Bolton Museum and Art Gallery, Le Mans Crescent, Bolton, Lancashire BL1 1SE. Telephone: 0204 22311 extension 2191.
Cambridge University Museum of Archaeology and Anthropology, Downing Street, Cambridge CB2 3DZ. Telephone: 0223 337733 or 333516.*
Liverpool Museum, William Brown Street, Liverpool L3 8EN. Telephone: 051-207 0001 or 5451.
Manchester Museum, The University of Manchester, Oxford Road, Manchester M13 9PL. Telephone: 061-273 3333.
Museum of Mankind (the Ethnography Department of the British Museum), 6 Burlington Gardens, London W1X 2EX. Telephone: 01-323 8043. Students' Room.*
Pitt Rivers Museum, South Parks Road, Oxford OX1 3PP. Telephone: 0865 270927.*
Royal Museum of Scotland, Chambers Street, Edinburgh EH1 1JF. Telephone: 031-225 7534.
Victoria and Albert Museum, Cromwell Road, South Kensington, London SW7 2RL. Telephone: 01-938 8500. Textile Study Room.*
Whitworth Art Gallery, The University of Manchester, Oxford Road, Manchester M15 6ER. Telephone: 061-273 4865.

Austria
Museum für Völkerkunde, Heldenplatz 3, Neue Hofburg, 1010 Vienna 1.

France
Musée de l'Homme, Palais de Chaillot, Place du Trocadéro, 75016 Paris.

Germany (West)
Museum für Völkerkunde, Staatliche Museen Preussischer Kulturbesitz, Arnimallee 23-27, 1000 Berlin 33.
Staatliches Museum für Völkerkunde, Maximilianstrasse 42, 8000 Munich 22, Bavaria.

Italy
Museo Preistorico Etnografico Luigi Pigorini, Via Lincoln 1, 00187 Rome.

Peru
Museo Amano, Calle Retiro 132-60, Miraflores, Lima.*
Museo Nacional de Antropología y Arqueología, Plaza Bolívar, Pueblo Libre, Lima.*

Spain
Museo de las Américas, Avenida de los Reyes Católicos, Ciudad Universitaria, Madrid 3.*

United States of America
American Museum of Natural History, 79th Street and Central Park West, New York, NY 10024.*
Brooklyn Museum, 188 Eastern Parkway, Brooklyn, New York, NY 11238.*
Dumbarton Oaks Research Library and Collection, 1703 32nd Street, NW, Washington DC 20007.
Metropolitan Museum of Art, 5th Avenue at 82nd Street, New York, NY 10028.*
Museum of the American Indian, Broadway at 155th Street, New York, NY 10032.*
Museum of Fine Arts, Huntington Avenue, Boston, Massachusetts 02115.
Robert H. Lowie Museum of Anthropology, 103 Kroeber Hall, University of California, Berkeley, California 94720.
Textile Museum, 2320 South Street, NW, Washington DC 20008.

9
Further reading

Peru
Bankes, George. *Peru before Pizarro.* Phaidon, 1977.
Hemming, John. *The Conquest of the Incas.* Macmillan, 1970; Penguin, 1983.

Textiles
Emery, Irene. *The Primary Structures of Fabrics: an Illustrated Classification.* The Textile Museum, Washington DC, 1966.

Peruvian textiles
Anton, Ferdinand. *Ancient Peruvian Textiles.* Thames and Hudson, 1987.
Cahlander, Adele. *Double Woven Treasures from Old Peru.* Dos Tejedoras, St Paul, Minnesota, 1985.
Cahlander, Adele. *Sling Braiding of the Andes.* Fiber Centre, Boulder, Colorado, 1980.
Fini, Moh. *The Weavers of Ancient Peru.* Tumi, London and Bath, 1985.
d'Harcourt, Raoul. *Textiles of Ancient Peru and Their Techniques* (edited by Grace Denny and Carolyn Osborne). University of Washington Press, Seattle, 1962. Several later reprintings.
Reid, J. *Textile Masterpieces of Ancient Peru.* Dover Publications, New York, 1986.
Rowe, Ann Pollard. *Warp Patterned Weaves of the Andes.* The Textile Museum, Washington DC, 1977.
Rowe, Ann Pollard. *Costumes and Featherwork of the Lords of Chimor: Textiles from Peru's North Coast.* The Textile Museum, Washington DC, 1984.
Wasserman, Tamara, and Hill, Jonathan. *Bolivian Indian Textiles: Traditional Design and Costume.* Dover Publications, New York, 1981.

Index

Page numbers in italic refer to illustrations

Peruvian Textiles